Kimiko Quest

Tim Kinard
Illustrated by Stan Gorman

Rigby®

A Harcourt Achieve Imprint

www.Rigby.com
1-800-531-5015

Literacy by Design Leveled Readers: *Kimiko Quest*

ISBN-13: 978-1-4189-3908-3
ISBN-10:   1-4189-3908-0

Printed in China
2 3 4 5 6 7 8 985 14 13 12 11 10 09 08

CONTENTS

Chapter 1
IN THE MAIL

Stella bounced up her front steps, jerking open the screen door to her family's farmhouse. Holding a letter from Iran in her hand, she stood looking at the unopened envelope and its unusual stamp.

She remembered the day she met Hesam, the boy who had sent her the letter. On that day she had leapt up her front steps and stared at something else she had gotten in the mail . . .

It was a package Stella had waited three long months for, and it contained the newest gaming system from the video game company, Kimiko Electronics. Stella tore into the package and gazed at the sleek beauty of her new Kimikovision video game. She held the Kimiko bodysuit, light as a feather, against her dress. It looked small, but Stella knew that the thin material containing the flexible wiring and microscopic motors would stretch easily to cover her in a shiny silver suit that would be her doorway into the most unbelievable, three-dimensional game ever played.

According to the advertisements, the bodysuit would sense Stella's every move and respond, allowing her to actually feel the imaginary world.

"Dad!"

Stella's father emerged from the kitchen and said, "What's all the noise about? Oh, I see you opened your package," he added, smiling.

"Can I start it up, Dad?" Stella begged.

"Mom is going to stay out in the field for a little while longer and fix one of the wind turbine generators, so I guess you can go ahead and play your game until she gets back."

"All right!" Stella exclaimed, kissing her dad's cheek and bounding up the stairs to her bedroom with her new gaming system clutched tightly in her hand.

In her room, Stella slipped into the sleek bodysuit, pulling the tight-fitting but weightless sensory controls over her head and face. As soon as Stella pulled the optic-goggles over her eyes, she felt as if she were floating.

"Unreal!" she cried delightedly.

A computerized voice answered, "Hello, Stella, we have received your information from your home computer."

Chapter 2
INTO THE GAME

"We are ready to start the game," the computerized voice continued soothingly, "and the weightless feeling you are now experiencing is a result of all the tiny micro-motors in your gaming suit. They are very sensitive and can cause your body to feel anything from complete weightlessness to the tiring effects of running, all while sitting still on your bedroom floor. Shall we begin?"

"You bet!" Stella replied excitedly.

An official-looking woman wearing a dark blue suit suddenly appeared before Stella's eyes, floating in the blackness.

"I'll be your guide until the game begins and you start your mission," she said in the same soothing voice.

Stella then felt the ground move beneath her feet, an unimaginable landscape appeared before her, and strange sounds and colors surrounded her. The temperature rose quickly—not hot, just warmer than the cool spring temperatures of the Iowa farm country.

Stella was amazed: what she saw, felt, and heard around her was unreal!

The sky—lime green—sparkled with ruby stars, and in the distance were steep, bright purple mountains that were unlike any Stella had ever seen on Earth. They rose on the horizon like three sharp teeth jutting straight up into the sky.

All around Stella could see what looked like enormous, orange, plastic flowers, each with three pointed petals. The ground she stood on was the gray color of an elephant's ear, but it was as smooth and shiny as glass.

Stella had to blink her eyes slowly a few times to get used to this new world's appearance because it was so different from the familiar landscape of the farm where she'd grown up. The farm seemed so far away now, even though Stella knew she was really still sitting in her bedroom

She noticed something floating in the sky above her; it was a great billowy shape, the color of pale blue cornflowers. Was it a cloud—or some sort of strange animal?

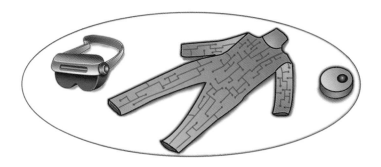

Chapter 3
THE BLUE PREDATORS

"Beautiful, isn't it?" a voice behind Stella said.

Stella whirled around and saw the middle-aged woman standing behind her.

The woman continued, "But don't let it fool you. It's hunting, and it sinks down to the surface of the planet and drapes its body over its victims, digesting them right there where it falls. It takes weeks to digest, then another few weeks for it to get light enough to float away to hunt again."

"What are they called?" Stella asked, amazed.

"I don't know because the beings in this world never thought to name each other, but we haven't got time for that now. Listen very carefully: this is your mission—you and the other players are a team . . ."

"Other players?" Stella interrupted, but the woman didn't respond.

" . . . and your mission is to find three things that will enable you to establish

a scientific research community on this imaginary planet."

The woman paused a moment, then went on, "You must find food, shelter, and a source of power for the scientists that will follow your team here. Here is a map of a few of the planet's surface features and, if you need to exit the game, just push the Panic Button on your suit. Good-bye, and good luck," and the woman flickered away as if someone had turned off an old-fashioned television set.

"Wait," Stella called, "what team? There's nobody else here!"

There was no answer, and when Stella looked around, she found she was standing alone in the strange landscape. She turned, as if she couldn't decide where to go, then took a step forward and stopped.

"I guess I should just turn off the game and see whether Mom needs help fixing the wind turbine. Now, where's that Panic Button?"

Stella looked down at her body and discovered what she hadn't noticed before: she was now wearing a spacesuit!

Chapter 4
THE PANIC BUTTON

The suit was made of some sort of white plastic with a pair of blue stripes extending the length of both Stella's arms and legs. Because of her helmet, she was looking at everything through a glass bubble.

"Cool," she said, when she noticed her pink space boots. "Oh, there's the button," and she reached up to the white button on her chest, which was clearly marked with letters that read "**PANIC**."

"See you later, weird world," Stella muttered.

Stella pushed the button and closed her eyes, ready to see the familiar colors and shapes of her bedroom. But when she opened her eyes, the sky was still lime green, and she could still see one of those blue, floating predators. She remained in the game, and although she pushed the button again . . . and again . . . and again, nothing happened.

"Hey, lady, come back–I'm stuck in here!" Stella shouted, not exactly scared, but certainly feeling uneasy.

"Uh, oh," she said, "I think this game's broken."

Chapter 5
THE TEAM

Suddenly Stella heard a crackling sound in her helmet, and a boy's voice said, "Hello? If you can hear me, and you're wearing one of these spacesuits that came with the new Kimikovision game, reach up and press the button on the side of your helmet that turns on your communicator."

Stella found the button, pushed it without hesitation, and said, "Can you hear me?"

"Awesome!" the boy's voice answered. "I thought I was alone out here."

Another voice said over the airwaves, "Hey, I can hear you, too!" It was another girl, and she said, "I can't get out of here and back to my breakfast in Japan."

Stella added, "I was just trying to get back to dinner at my house in the United States, too."

The boy's voice said, "Same here—I was just trying to turn the game off, so I could go back to bed. It's way past my bedtime in Iran. Where are you?"

"I don't know," the other girl said. "I can see a picture of three purple cones, on my map, and off to my left I can see three huge purple cones."

Stella replied, "I can see those off to my right, so I must be on the other side of them."

"Well, I'm standing right next to them," said the boy, "and they are definitely huge."

"Maybe we should meet at these cones and try to figure out what to do to get out of this game and go home," continued the boy.

"I agree," said Stella.

"Me, too," said the girl from Japan, adding, "See you in a minute."

Stella started walking to the purple mountain-looking things she could see on her map as well as in the distance, and wondered how far they really were: "It's hard to tell how big anything is in this weird landscape," she thought.

"Hey, what are your names?" Stella suddenly asked.

"My name is Hesam," said the boy.

"And mine's Reina," said the other girl, adding, "You both speak Japanese so well."

Hesam answered, "Japanese? I thought you two were speaking Farsi, the language I speak in Iran."

"That's funny," Stella said, "I thought we were all speaking English!"

"The game must come with a translator," Reina noted.

"Cool!" they all said at the same time.

Chapter 6
AT THE PURPLE MOUNTAINS

Stella, Reina, and Hesam walked in silence for a while, but Stella wasn't sure how long. Finally, when the three purple cones were towering before her, she saw a glint of light reflected off something not too far away.

"Hey," Hesam exclaimed, "I think I can see one of you!"

"I think I can see you, too!" cried Stella.

"I can see you both now!" Reina exclaimed.

They all ran to meet one another, hugging through their spacesuits, even though they'd never met.

"Look at these things!" Reina said, staring up at the smooth, gleaming, purple cones that stretched up into the sky.

"Yeah, from far away I hadn't noticed those little ledges that spiral up them like giant staircases—it's so cool," Hesam added.

"You know what's really cool?" Stella interjected. "We all just hugged each other . . . and we're really in our houses in three completely different parts of the world!"

"Yeah, that really is cool!" Hesam and Reina agreed.

"But . . . " Stella continued, "I'm a little nervous that our Panic Buttons didn't work. I'm starting to feel like I might really panic if we can't get out of here and go back to our families."

They all nodded, standing in silence, wondering what to do next.

Suddenly Reina had a plan, saying, "You know, when I started the game, there was a computerized woman that told me I needed to find three things—shelter, food, and a source of power. Maybe if we find those three things, the game will finish and we can all go home and call Kimiko Electronics and tell them their game needs to be fixed!"

"It's worth a shot," Hesam said.

"I agree," said Stella. "Well, what should we try to find first?"

Chapter 7
FAMILIAR POWER IN A STRANGE LAND

Stella, Reina, and Hesam stood together wondering what to do next.

"I know," Reina said, "let's climb those purple cones! We can walk along the edge of the cones and see if we can get any ideas from looking at the land around us."

The other two agreed and they each started up a narrow spiraling ledge, walking slowly and carefully for what seemed like hours. In the distance, the kids could see a change in the surface of the planet.

It looked as if all the pink lemonade on Earth had spilled out to their left. Looking on her map, Reina could see the pink splotch to the west of the purple cones upon which they were standing. On the map the pink was dotted with yellow, however, and she couldn't see anything yellow from where she stood. She started to say something.

Stella heard Reina's voice over the radio of her helmet, but she couldn't hear what she said.

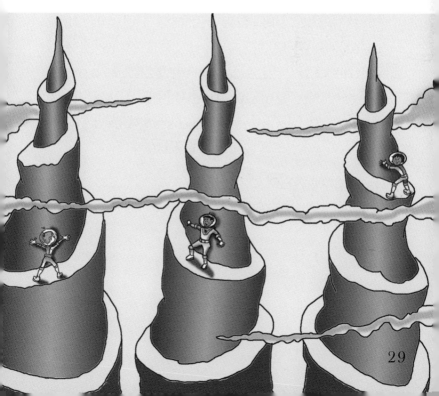

"I can't hear you!" yelled Stella, because her helmet was howling with the sound of the air outside.

"That's it!" exclaimed Hesam. "It's windy up here–that's why it's so loud, and that's what moves those great blue predators through the sky."

"Of course! Why didn't I think of that earlier? It's just like on our farm back home," thought Stella. "We can use the wind as a source of power!"

"We can make a wind turbine!" Stella cried out, yelling over the howling wind.

"Let's get down from here before we get blown down and start figuring out how to do it," Reina exclaimed.

The team descended the peaks as quickly as possible without risking falling off the narrow ledges. As the kids reached the bottom, Stella looked around at the stunning scene—the great orange flowers stood out dramatically against the lime green sky.

Chapter 8
PLAYING FOR SURVIVAL

Stella suddenly called out, "Hey, those plants that look like plastic flowers–I noticed them before, but I wasn't thinking about home, just about this weird planet."

"What about them?" called Hesam.

"They look like the turbines on our windmills back home. We could turn the petals into fans that catch the wind and create power!"

"Awesome!" said Reina. "And I was thinking that we should go check out that big pink area over there next."

Reina gazed around her and said, "My home in Japan is by the ocean, and almost everything you could need can be found in the water. I bet this planet is no different, and something tells me that the pink stuff is this weird world's version of an ocean. Maybe we can find food and shelter over there."

When they finally reached the ground, they started off toward the pink splotch they saw on their maps.

"We'll collect those big orange flowers on the way; they seem to be everywhere," said Stella.

"Well, we already found the source of power. I think we're pretty good at this game," said Hesam, "even though we're not playing it for fun right now."

"Yeah," Reina added, "we're playing for survival!"

At that instant Stella noticed a shadow fall across Reina's helmet. They all three looked up and saw a great blue blob descending upon them!

"Run!" Hesam screamed.

"It's one of those predators!" shouted Stella.

"Hurry!" cried Reina.

It was just over their heads, looming huge, and coming right for them. Stella knew they couldn't outrun it. There was no way out!

35

Just then a new voice crackled in over their headsets.

"I'm so terribly sorry," it said, "there seems to have been a glitch in the game's programming."

Suddenly, the blue predator flickered once, then disappeared.

Chapter 9
RETURNING HOME

The lime green sky turned as dark as space, and the jutting purple cones faded into darkness. Stella, Reina, and Hesam were floating again, and suspended before them was the same woman who had introduced Stella to this mysterious world hours before.

"We received your Panic Button call," the woman said, "but we were unable to shut down the game. However, the malfunction has been corrected."

"You mean we can go home?" Stella, Reina, and Hesam cried together.

"Yes, you may; you will be returning in 30 seconds."

"Wait," Stella shouted, "will I ever see my new friends again?"

"Of course," the game's voice said, "you can all meet back here each time you play. Just remember the ID numbers on your teammates' spacesuits."

I don't think I'll be returning to this world," said Stella. "Let's just give each other our addresses and write letters when we get back home.

Stella, Reina, and Hesam laughed, exchanged addresses, and listened as the computer finished its countdown, " . . . 3 . . . 2 . . . 1 . . . "

Suddenly Stella couldn't see a thing. At first she started to panic, but then she remembered she was wearing the Kimikovision suit and took off her optic-goggles.

Stella could see her room and the sky—the *blue* sky—outside her window. She stood up and started to run outside, but then she remembered something: she stopped at her desk and wrote down her two new friends' addresses before she forgot them.

"I'll talk to you two again," she said to the paper with Hesam and Reina's addresses on it, "I'm sure of it!" Then she ran downstairs calling, "Dad, you'll never guess what just happened!"